The LOVE of Attraction

Tested Secrets to Let Go of Fear-Based Mindsets, Activate LOA Faster, and Start Manifesting Your Desires!

Law of Attraction Short Reads, Book 5

By Elena G. Rivers

Copyright Elena G. Rivers © 2020

All rights reserved. No part of this publication may be reproduced, stored in a retrieval system, or transmitted, in any form or by any means, electronic, mechanical, photocopying, recording, or otherwise, without the prior written permission of the author and the publishers.

The scanning, uploading, and distribution of this book via the Internet or via any other means without the permission of the author is illegal and punishable by law. Please purchase only authorized electronic editions and do not participate in or encourage electronic piracy of copyrighted materials.

Elena G. Rivers © Copyright 2020 - All rights reserved.

ISBN: 978-1-80095-059-7

Legal Notice:

This book is copyright protected. It for personal use only.

Disclaimer Notice:

Please note the information contained in this book is for inspirational and entertainment purposes only. Every attempt has been made to provide accurate, up to date, and completely reliable information. No warranties of any kind are expressed or implied. Readers acknowledge that the author is not engaging in the rendering of legal, financial, health, medical, or professional advice. By reading this book, the reader agrees that under no circumstances are we responsible for any losses, direct or indirect, which are incurred as a result of the use of the information contained within this book, including, but not limited to, errors, omissions, or inaccuracies.

The information provided in this book is for entertainment purposes only. If you are struggling with serious problems, including chronic illness, mental instability, or legal issues, please consult with your local registered health care or legal professional as soon as possible. This book is not a substitute for professional or legal advice

Contents

The LOVE of Attraction 1

Why the LOVE of Attraction? 7

Why It's ALL About Mindfully Mastering the Basics 12

Pillar#1 Your Authentic Alignment 30

Pillar #2 Your Desire Must be Authentic and So Must Be Your Energy 31

Pillar#3 Process Negative Energy Fast 32

Pillar#4 Love vs Fear-Based Mindset 34

Pillar 5# Know Your Authentic Frequency 38

Pillar#6 Release Wanting and Doubting 40

Pillar#7 When Focusing on "Why Not's" Can Be Good for You 42

Secret #1 Realize When Your Subconscious Mind Goes Against You and Change the Disk 46

Secret #2 Do You Choose to Feel Light or Heavy? 52

Secret #3 Choosing Your Vibration 55

Secret#4 The Power of the Why Behind the Why 62

Secret#5 Releasing Low Vibrations and Using Certainty for Your Highest Good 65

Secret #6 Not All Negative Programming Is Really Negative 72

Secret#7 Release This Invisible Manifestation Killer 82

Secret#8 The Liberating Essence of Letting Go . 86

Secret#9 Your Healthy, Love-Based Boundaries 92

Secret #10 When Making Mistakes is Important If You Want to Attract Abundance 106

Personal Message from Elena 110

Free LOA Newsletter + Bonus Gift 112

More Books by Elena G. Rivers 114

Why the LOVE of Attraction?

You can't fail with the power of love. Because love can create *only* good things in your life. So, if you're tired of negativity and feel ready to release what's no longer serving you so that you can start living your dream life, you've come to the right place.

You found this book for a reason! It doesn't matter if you've read any of my other books. It doesn't matter if you've studied or practiced LOA before. And it doesn't matter where you're from, how old you are and what you do for a living.

Anyone can unleash the power of love to release negative mindsets and energy patterns that block their positive manifestations.

This is why I'm writing this book! In the last few months, I've been getting signs from the Universe that made it clear I should write it. The signs would come consistently almost every day. Most readers who were reaching out to me seeking LOA guidance already knew a lot about it. They learned different manifestation methods and had some success with them. They even knew the Law of Attraction mistakes to avoid. Yet, for some reason, they still felt a little bit blocked. Judging from the way they wrote to me and asked questions, it became evident to me what the missing puzzle in their LOA practice was.

To take their manifestations to the next level, all they had to do was to embrace the power of love and authenticity. They had to use that power to get rid of all the negative mindsets and beliefs.

This book is short for a reason. It's not about how much time you spend reading (unless you really enjoy reading and it makes you feel good), but more about how you read and the time you take to apply what you've learned.

The introduction that follows will help you understand the fundamental pillars of this simple, love-based system. Then, we will jump into ten tested loved-based secrets to get you out of the negativity and into the spiral of positive manifestations.

The main thing I want you to understand is that *everything* you've been exposed to so far *is mostly fear-based.*

For example, what you hear on the news, advertising on social media, conversations you may have heard from other people. Most messages your mind receives are probably fear-based.

It's no wonder that our minds are so filled with fear. Even positive, spiritual people like us can still hold many fear-based mindsets.

And there is nothing wrong with realizing that. Conscious self-development is a journey that never ends. I release negativity almost every day!

If you've read any of my other books, you already know that I'm all for positivity. However, I'm not a big fan of fake positivity. I don't subscribe to burying your head in the sand, pretending all is good while actually feeling bad.

Genuine positivity and freedom emerge when we face our fear-based mindsets and energies while embracing a mindful state of awareness. Then, we can observe what's going on around us and mindfully choose a different, more aligned, and positive response. With a positive response from within, we change on a deeper level. Then, we have the power to influence our reality.

This is what this little book is designed to help you with. I highly recommend you get your notebook ready and do the exercises as you read. I also recommend you read this book several times. Every time you read the same book, the way you perceive it is different because every time you read it, your energy shifts.

So, without any further ado, let's do this!

As I already mentioned, we will start off with an introduction to understand how this love-based manifestation formula works.

Then, we will dive into ten powerful long-term manifestation secrets.

You can read this book in one sitting; it should take one or two hours max. Or, you can take your time and go through each secret every day. It's up to you!

I'm very excited for you and feel very privileged to be writing this book for you. My purpose in life is to help raise the vibration of the planet. I fulfill my mission mainly through writing, and I'm very grateful for curious, ambitious souls like you! Ambitious, spiritually curious people who are ready to take meaningful action, dive deeper, do the inner work, and become the change they want to see on this planet.

"You must be the change you want to see in the world." – by Gandhi

"You can have everything in life you want if you will just help other people get what they want." – by Zig Ziglar

"People who have great lives think and talk about what they love more than what they don't love. And people who are struggling, think and talk about what they don't love more than what they do love." – by Rhonda Byrne

"Working on our own consciousness is the most important thing that we are doing at any moment, and being Love is the supreme creative act." – by Ram Dass

"The Law of Attraction or the Law of Love...they are one and the same." – by Charles Haanel

"If we look at the world with a love of life, the world will reveal its beauty to us." – by Daisaku Ikeda

Why It's ALL About Mindfully Mastering the Basics

Do you know the secrets of the most successful football coaches? It's simple - they focus on the basic stuff before anything else. And even after getting into more advanced techniques, they always remind their students about the basics through consistent and mindful repetition.

They make sure their teams embrace the basics to such an extent that it becomes automatic to them.

For example, a football player can learn a myriad of new techniques to run faster and whatnot. However, if they can't even tie their shoes properly or have no clue how to prevent injury, they won't be successful.

Weird example, I know. But I see this all the time in LOA or self-help community. People are looking for some magic pill or for something new.

The truth is that it's not about how much we know. Yes, knowledge is power. I don't discredit the desire for more knowledge. But, what's even more power is your expertise in action. You want your ability to turn into your inner wisdom. So that all your efforts, thoughts, and feelings are aligned with what you desire.

To get to that level, it's all about mindful repetition of what you already know. Even when it feels a bit boring.

And trust me, I learned this the hard way!

It's up to you to make it exciting by using your imagination. Why am I telling you this?

Well, have you considered grounding yourself before diving into this material? Do you ever ground yourself? And do you ground yourself every day?

If you don't because you've never heard of it, and you don't know how, well, you will start in just a minute. But, if you already know what grounding is, but you don't do it, use it as a signal from the Universe to ground yourself more often. Don't be one of those negative, sarcastic "LOA-ers" who just complain about everything they read with: "Oh, nothing new here."

I used to be one of those sarcastic "I already know it all" individuals too. I struggled with weight loss for years, and I just kept reading more fad diet books. I would criticize all of them. *Nothing new here!* It was only when someone called me bitter and fat that I actually decided to do something about my weight. Instead of looking for a new diet plan or a magic pill, I focused on the basics. I stopped eating fast food and drinking soda. I quit sugar and began walking every day. That little lifestyle change alone helped me lose weight! A simple, common-sense diet and moderate exercise.

Now, I'm very grateful for my weight loss struggle because it taught me how to be a better person and release sarcasm. Now, I really appreciate anyone who puts themselves out there with any material designed to help people with something.

Even if I'm already familiar with their information, or it's not really for me, I still appreciate their efforts. Why? Because now, I operate from a place of love, not fear, criticism, and jealousy. And so, even if I'm to give someone honest feedback that I believe can help them improve, I do it kindly and with respect.

We're not necessarily looking for the new. Instead, we're unleashing something that deep inside we know is good for us. We make a mindful decision to do what we already know, again and again, to use it as a personal transformation tool.

This is why I politely ask you to please ground yourself first to get the most out of this book.

(And everything you read or do, really.)

One of my best friends is a professional saleswoman who did very well in her career. She grounds herself before most of her sales calls. Her energy is better because of her simple grounding rituals, and she gets much better results with her work.

I ground myself before all my writing sessions, and now I never experience the so-called *writer's block*. When you ground yourself, are calm, and operate from a place of love and authenticity, there is no such thing as *a block*.

Doing your work feels right and natural—no reason to block anything.

OK, so let's ground! I'm here right now grounding myself with you!

Grounding Exercise
(Just Do It and Please Don't Complain You Already Know This!)

Take off your shoes. Relax Your Body.

Close your eyes.

Start breathing consciously.

Breathe in for 3-5 seconds, hold your breath for 3-5 seconds, and then breathe out for 3-5 seconds.

Repeat several times until you start feeling relaxed.

Keep breathing consciously at whatever pace is convenient for you.

Now, get in a flow state by imagining light from the sky, beautiful, warm yellow light, enter your body through your head. You can feel the light warming your head and moving down and down, illuminating all your body.

Now, the light reaches your feet, going deeper and deeper. Visualize the light diving deep into the earth and becoming a grounding root.
Finish off your grounding process by saying thank you, thank you, thank you.

This short exercise shouldn't take more than five minutes. I highly recommend you do it whenever you need to enter a peaceful state of mind or raise your awareness and learn new things better and faster.

I want you to remember that this yellow light is always there for you. Whenever you need to wash off any negative feelings or experiences; whenever you need to make a decision or do something important but feel unfocused - get back to doing this exercise.

Love is the creative force of everything in the Universe.

And it's the only force that can permanently take you from fear, negativity, and darkness to manifesting your dream life, almost on autopilot. It's not even about how many manifestation methods you know or do. It's about who you are and who you become. Your energy and vibration are everything. When you turn to love and embody love, you will automatically manifest everything that you love.

Before I discovered the Love of Attraction, my life was a mess. Yes, I kept manifesting, but only negative things. I manifested a very abusive relationship. I lacked the courage to leave because I felt scared of being alone and feared that nobody would want me because I was too old.

I manifested a job and then my own business that most people would envy. Unfortunately, it wasn't aligned with my passions and strengths and would always burn me out.

Even with a good salary, I always lacked money. I felt scared because some unexpected expenses would always manifest, and I couldn't get out of debt.

I couldn't experience vibrant health either. Even though I tried to stay healthy, my stressful life eventually led me to resort to alcohol, fast food, tobacco, and other substances to numb myself. I couldn't stick to any self-care plan. And as you already know, I struggled with weight loss. It felt like all the old energies and emotions I couldn't release kept accumulating as excess weight.

It wasn't until I decided to dive deep to examine the root cause of all my problems that a sad but very liberating realization came:

Elena, you're living your life and making all decisions from a place of fear, not a place of love. You're in the mindset and energy of escaping from what you don't want. You keep focusing on the negative. Therefore, you negatively activate the Law of Attraction. Focus on love. Make decisions from a place of love and love yourself to start attracting people and circumstances that love you.

Then, I took meaningful action and decided to work on myself using love-based concepts of the Law of Attraction, which I now call the LOVE of Attraction.

Just a few months after my decision, I transformed every area of my life. I was no longer in an abusive relationship; I found my way out and was happily single.

At that time, I wanted to focus on healing myself and doing the inner work before repeating my old patterns of "trying to find someone to not feel alone." So, being single is what I wanted back then. And eventually, I did manifest my soul mate and moved to a beautiful island in the Atlantic.

I found the courage to finally be myself and follow my passion with love and confidence. My new energy opened several new professional gates for me, such as manifesting an unexpected deal with an audiobook company. Now, I love the work I'm doing, and even though I work hard, I no longer feel burned out. It all feels very aligned, and I'm honored to be fulfilling my life mission and purpose every day.

My health improved because I embraced the power of love and self-care. Instead of taking misaligned actions from the fear of getting overweight or sick, I took action from a place of love for healthy living. It felt natural to me to eat a whole-food diet and highly vibrational foods. That gave me more energy and conviction to carry on.

And, most importantly, I began attracting super high vibe people into my life. This is what I call *true abundance*- when all areas of your life are aligned and complement one another.

After all, would you like to manifest vast amounts of money but end up sick, unhappy, or unfulfilled? Of course not. You want abundance in all areas of your life.

So, take a few minutes now to reflect. You, too, can design your ideal life from a place of love, not fear. Yes, there's always one area of life that might need more attention.

But, staying in balance is essential. You want to create abundance! Not only in terms of dollars made. Your emotional bank account balance also matters.

Design a vision for your dream life now and create a short mission statement (one to three sentences) for each area of your life:

My health

Example:
-I choose to eat healthy foods that give me unstoppable energy and vibrant health.

-I love foods that nourish my body.

-I'm blessed to indulge in long baths and beautiful walks in nature.

My Passion/ Purpose / Fulfillment
Example:

-I feel so grateful I found my calling in life.

-I'm even more grateful I can do my passion for a living.

-My purpose sets my soul on fire!

My relationships

Example:

-*I get amazingly well with my family, friends, and the man/woman of my dreams.*

-*We're all happy people; we love and support each other.*

-*I attract high vibe people into my life.*

Money/finance

Example:

-*I'm open to receiving.*

-*I mindfully create new opportunities and new sources of income.*

-*Money is energy, and I'm energy; therefore, I attract money into my life.*

Spirituality

Example:

-I experience unforgettable spiritual moments in my life.

- I feel loved and cared for by the Universe/God/ Higher Power.

That was the first step. Get back to it to remind yourself what's yet to come and how amazing your life can get.

Everything happens for a reason, and there are no coincidences. We attracted each other. After experiencing my own personal transformation, I made it my mission to help others do the same. Our planet needs more love and more loved-based people. And so, my intention is to awaken those who are still in a fear-based mindset so that they can awaken to the creative power of love.

But you must be open to receiving help. You see, so many people I know asked me for help because they saw my transformation. But when I explained what I did, they began saying:

Oh, you just got lucky.

Or:

It's because you were in the right place at the right time.

Or:

It's because you were born rich.

Which is not true. My transformation did not happen by accident. And I wasn't born into a wealthy or influential family either.

What happened is that I took concrete steps to change my actions, feelings, responses, and thoughts. As a curious mind, I reverse-engineered what worked and created my own Love of Attraction formula.

Those who asked me for help and were open to receiving support didn't discredit my transformation as some coincidence. Instead, they happily followed the exact same process, in their own way. As a result, they, too, could transform all areas of their lives.

Take a look at your dream life vision you've designed in the previous exercise. Ask yourself, do you really desire to attract all that? Would you be open to making your vision a reality or get closer to your goals in the next few months?

If the answer is yes, keep reading and applying. This guide is not designed for passive reading, and I can't help those who are skeptical and aren't willing to follow the steps I outlined.

I still remember how embarrassing it felt...it was my birthday. I invited some friends over. I went to the store to buy some food and drinks for my party, and my credit card got declined. I had to leave with nothing. I can still remember how embarrassing it felt! All those people at the supermarket were staring at me.

Then, I discovered I didn't even have enough gas to drive back home. I had to ask friends for help. I felt ashamed to share my situation with my family or partner. All I could attract was debt. And it was back then when I hit my rock bottom that I just knew I had to change myself and my energy.

LOA and manifestation saved me. To be more precise, the Love of Attraction saved me.

Everything has its vibrational energy. This page has a vibration, and so does your hand. Your thoughts and emotions are energy, and they also stimulate the release of neurohormones, which send signals to your brain.

The grey matter, the part of the brain that controls your emotions, impulses, and thoughts, is something we can influence, using the positive power of love.

We can control our emotional responses to external stimuli and events. In other words-we can send positive, loved-based frequencies towards our desires so that we don't get pushed off course with misaligned frequencies.

For example, if someone is rude to you, what is your response? Are you angry the entire day? Or do you allow yourself a few minutes to process that negativity and then consciously take meaningful action to get back to a positive vibration? Do you deviate your energy just because something didn't go well? Or do you decide to move on because you know that even if things don't go as planned, the Universe knows what's right for your long-term wellbeing?

When you decide to focus on conscious decisions, you become a conscious person. As a conscious person, you create conscious life. You design your life just like you already did!

It's all about understanding and then removing old programs and blueprints that might be leading you to negative manifestations. Awareness is so important.

There are seven crucial pillars in this process. We will have a look at each of them so that you understand how it works. Then, we will be diving into ten Love of Attraction secrets. But before we do, it's so important you understand the framework! Mindset is everything!

Pillar#1 Your Authentic Alignment

Understand that if you choose so, everything happens for you, not to you. Sometimes things don't go our way because there's something better waiting for us. The Universe knows what's good for us.

Sometimes it just wants to test us or send us challenging circumstances for us to transform. For example, I'm grateful for all the hardship I'd experienced. I see it as a blessing because this is how I hit rock bottom and decided to transform. Many people experience something very similar.

Ask yourself, how do you react when things don't go your way? For example, you wanted to manifest a new job or promotion but didn't get it. You can choose to feel scared or pessimistic: *why me? Why can others do it and I can't? What's wrong with me?*

Or, you can choose to affirm to the Universe: *Thank you for testing me, I'm still here, and I know I'm on the right path. Thank you for the reminder!*

Pillar #2 Your Desire Must be Authentic and So Must Be Your Energy

Very often, we set goals that aren't even ours but come from other people. In other words, we want to manifest and achieve to make other people happy or to show off. I've been there so many times, and for so long, I had no idea I was blocking my own happiness.

The honest truth is that with no authenticity, there is no alignment. And with no alignment, we can't manifest positive outcomes. No matter how hard we try.

Whatever it is that you set to manifest, it must be your goal. Suppose you want something simply because everyone else has it, and you don't want to be left behind. In that case, you are following trends, not your true authentic desires. Keep asking your higher self: *is this what I truly want? Will it make me happy?*

Pillar#3 Process Negative Energy Fast

What do you do when you encounter a negative block, person, or situation? For example, someone said something rude to you. How much time do you need to let go? Five seconds, five hours, five days, fifty years?

The sooner you let go, the better. Understand that rude people harm themselves, not you.

You can choose to stay out of their negative vibration.

Also, by doing the inner work described in this guide, you will be raising your vibration, attracting more positive people, and automatically moving away from fear.

The art of letting go is so crucial. Whenever I experience something negative, I allow myself some time to process and release it.

With practice and firm intention, it becomes automatic. The more you hold onto negative things that someone did to you, the more you harm yourself. You keep replaying the negative loop and experiencing the same negative vibration over and over again.

And when it comes to rude people and their negativity, well, it's theirs. Choose to hold your space. Visualize yourself having a nice shower in a waterfall. Keep breathing and affirming: *I fly so high that I can only see positivity.*

Pillar#4 Love vs. Fear-Based Mindset

Jessica desires to manifest a beach house because she loves the vibe of the ocean. She loves the seagulls and surfing. She feels free, waking up near the ocean. So, she manifests from a place of love. For her, manifesting a beach house fully aligns with who she is.

However, Mary wants to manifest a beach house because one of her siblings lives in one. Her parents keep praising her sibling and their successful professional career and how they could afford such a place. Mary doesn't feel appreciated by her parents. So, she thinks that by manifesting a beach house, she too will get attention and appreciation. She imagines how it would feel to invite some of her friends to her new home and how they would envy her such a success. Maybe she could even get a bigger house than her sibling.

Needless to say, Jessica manifests from a loved-based mindset and Mary from a fear-based mindset. Which manifestation do you think will have a happy ending? By a happy ending, I refer to a lifetime of joy, fulfillment, and abundance.

I used to be so similar to Mary! I was in constant fear and wanted to prove to others that I was worthy, smart, and significant. Yet, I couldn't believe it myself. I wasn't myself. My goals weren't mine.

So, ask yourself, do you want to manifest from a place of love or fear? Misaligned mindsets come from anxiety and other people's opinions. Don't allow them into your space.

Don't hold onto the stuck energy of trying to please other people and manifest to show off. Stuck energy leads to bad circumstances. Don't manifest from fear; fear isn't yours. Be aware that fear-based goals may hide in superficial prestige, appreciation, and desperate attempts to make other people like you.

When you think about what you desire to manifest, you should feel light, not heavy. Too much heavy energy indicates that what you wish to manifest is not truly yours, or you're not ready for it yet. For the time being, you should prepare yourself by doing something else.

Your emotions hold super strong frequency. They eventually manifest into a physical reality by going from fluid to dense. Suppose you focus on positive emotions and use all their power. In that case, you will automatically manifest more positive things into your life.

Unfortunately, most people use this formula but with negative emotions and get stuck in a never-ending negative loop.

Pillar 5# Know Your Authentic Frequency

Some people don't study LOA and manifestation, yet they always manifest incredible things. Why is that?

Well, some people have this natural, positive energy, and they've been filled with it for a long time. They just align, take action, and get what they desire. And, most importantly, they are authentic, and they know what they want. They don't confuse the Universe.

In contrast, some people, such as my old self, have no idea about their authentic desires and try to manifest to please other people. Or they desire things because it's a trend and everyone is doing this or having that.

Be that simple, authentic, and aligned person. It's a choice. Less is more. You can start manifesting one desire at a time if you fully embrace the energy of positive emotion and authentic love.

Be true to yourself and always speak your truth from a place of kindness, consideration, and respect for others whose truth might be different. It's not that we all have to believe in the same things. It's all about allowing yourself and others to live in peace.

Pillar #6 Release Wanting and Doubting

If you struggle with manifesting, chances are your energy is split in two or more directions.

For example, maybe you desire to manifest your own brand. You want to be a revolutionary coach, have an online presence, and attract amazing clients.

A business mentor advises you to start a YouTube channel to share your truth, provide value, and attract those who seek guidance. Or perhaps you're advised to start running Facebook ads.

Yet, you're scared...what if your friends and family see your videos or advertisements and they don't like them? And so, your energy is split.

We often split our energy subconsciously, we want something consciously, but deep inside, we fear it. For example, you may think you want money (deliberately). Still, your subconscious mind rebels thinking it's evil, and you might lose your friends. And so, since all your actions are led by your subconscious, you start sabotaging yourself.

No judgment here; negative results are just feedback. They are not even that negative if we use them correctly- as a motivation to shed light on the darkness while releasing old beliefs that no longer serve us. You don't fail, you succeed, or you learn. Treat unfavorable circumstances as data. Imagine you're a mad LOA detective or scientist; well, now you know what not to do!

Pillar #7 When Focusing on "Why not's" Can Be Good for You

Go back to your dream life exercise. If you're not living it right now, ask yourself, why can't you have it? Did someone say something in the past, making you feel unworthy?

For example, for years, I struggled in business because my ex-partner once told me:

So, you want to start your own business? You're a cute wannabie. Yeah, right, like one of those femalepreneur lady bosses posing on social media. I saw one offering a webinar today. Laughable! They know nothing about business, and you know even less than they do. You're so cute talking about it, but you're not cut out for business. Business is men's stuff. And what when we settle down and have kids? You're not gonna have time for your business anyway".

And for years, it was my story, a man told me this, and I chose to believe it. I didn't even consciously remember I made it my belief.

So, if something similar happened to you, release it now! Everything is possible with the love of attraction because love is the highest power that can arrange everything for your highest good, happiness, and abundance!

Use the following questions:
-what do you want?
-why do you think you can't have it now?
-is it your belief or rule or someone else's
-where did you get those rules?
-does this old baggage empower you in any way?

Misaligned energy is used to protect your old ways that perhaps were helpful in the past. But now, unfortunately, they close new channels of abundance and happiness for you.

Keep affirming to the Universe that you're ready for and open to new possibilities and new avenues of receiving for the highest good of all.

Now that you understand the foundation of love versus fear-based mindsets and how to use their power to activate LOA while releasing negativity, let's jump into our love-based secrets.

Each secret focuses on a specific technique, question, or exploration to turn your life into a never-ending flow of love and abundance in all areas of your life.

Secret #1 Realize When Your Subconscious Mind Goes Against You and Change the Disk

Kate is a gorgeous woman. Yet, she always struggled with her self-image. She was obsessed with her looks, always looking for ways to "improve" and look better.

Yet, whenever someone complimented her, she didn't take it seriously; she thought they were ironic or trying to get to her.

She struggled with relationships too. For some reason, the men she liked would always choose other women (who, for some reason, weren't that astonishingly beautiful). Everyone would say that poor Kate simply "didn't have luck" in love. And that all those men were stupid for not wanting to be with her.

The negative pattern would continue. Kate tried to look more beautiful (even though she was already beautiful). But, for some reason, she kept repelling all the men she liked. She was living a life of loneliness and not feeling good enough.

Eventually, she embarked on a self-development journey and learned how to dive deep. She wanted to find the root cause of all her issues.

It turned out that when she was a little girl, a family member called her ugly.

And that event stayed in her subconscious mind for years. At first, it was there, like a dormant volcano. But, when Kate was a teenager, she began obsessing with her looks, realizing that she needed compliments from other people to feel worthy.

The negative pattern got re-activated and haunted her for years. Only when she understood the fear-based mechanism that was driving her for so many years could she do something about it.

She could finally, as I like to put it, change the disk.

Or, in other words, she could change her behavior. She could accept the fact she didn't need to prove anything to anyone. She was already naturally beautiful and could own her beauty. She no longer had to resort to plastic surgeries and enhancements to "keep improving." She could be herself. As such, she attracted an amazing man into her life.

What about you and your old disk? What negative patterns do you hold about your:

-looks
-qualifications
-finances
-relationships

What is the fear-based program that's controlling your life and your behaviors?

Are you ready to let it go for good? There's time to hold on, and there's time to let go. When letting go of any negative pattern or fear-based belief, embrace self-love as much as you can.

It's common for many people (and I've been there myself too) to feel angry, guilty, or even stupid when thinking about their old behaviors.

Embrace the power of mindfulness and the present moment. Take a few deep breaths. At this moment, you are safe and empowered. You write your own story. You design your life.

Keep affirming:

I'm now safe.

There's time to hold on, and there's time to let go.

Hey, my subconscious mind, I want to thank you for holding on to this belief (that I wasn't good enough, was fat, wasn't beautiful enough).

I know you were trying to protect me.

But now, it's time for me to let go. From now on, I choose to believe that I'm good enough, I'm worthy of love, abundance, and financial freedom.

For many people, this is the missing link to the Law of Attraction. Creating your own affirmations that make friends with your subconscious mind.

Thank your subconscious mind for trying to protect you for so many years. Kindly let it know that now times have changed - you're safe, and you can now choose a different set of beliefs, therefore acting differently.

At the same time, many people choose positive thinking, which is excellent. However, they are still driven by their old behaviors because they haven't made friends with their subconscious mind. They haven't changed the disk, or in other words, they haven't changed their actions and how they react to different situations.

This was my story, too, for so many years. Yes, I felt a bit better because of "trying to stay positive." But I was still the old me, trying to prove myself to others all the time because I didn't feel worthy. Like I mentioned previously, an ex-partner of mine ridiculed my ideas of having my own business. And so, later, all my actions were driven by the fact that I wanted to show him and others that I could succeed in business (even if the price was to go against my own happiness).

Fear-based motivations are very short-sighted. Yes, they can help us get started on a new path. But they will not allow us to keep going while living happy, balanced, and abundant lives.

Ask yourself if you're ready to change your behavior and how you react to different situations. The Love of Attraction is not only about how you think but also about how you act. Suppose you really change the way you think. In that case, it means you automatically become a different person and change the way you act, therefore creating a new reality.

Secret #2 Do You Choose to Feel Light or Heavy?

You have your internal compass, your intuition. You are the only one who can make accurate decisions in alignment with who you are.

Before we dive deeper, please note, the purpose of this section is not to make you feel bad. I don't want you to go on any guilt trips such as: "Oh no, all the decisions or most of the decisions I made in my life were made out of fear."

Here's the truth: we all made most of our life decisions based on fear because this is how we were programmed. There's no point in feeling bad. If anything, you can choose to feel liberated because now you can stick to love-based mindsets and change your life.

An authentic decision is when you feel light. You know you are choosing something in alignment with your true desires. For example, you decide to follow your passion and sign up for a certified program to become a life coach. You follow your intuition. You just know you're doing the right thing.

At the same time, if you decide to make other people happy (even though you feel totally out of alignment), you might experience heaviness.

Heaviness is caused by fear-based mindsets. Perhaps you make a decision totally against yourself because you were told that things "have always been done in a certain way." Or maybe your decision is automatic; you don't even give it much thought because you have no idea what's driving you.

If you want to live a happy life, most of your decisions need to be made out of love and in alignment with your authentic goals and aspirations.

I use the word "most" because I'm a realist. And I know that not everything is black or white. For example, in some cases, we need a little bit of fear-based motivation to get started on taking action or to realize we need to change. There's nothing wrong with short-term fear-based measures if they are meant to lead us to our light. Everyone is on a different journey.

Simultaneously, to get into alignment and follow our inner light, sometimes we need to face our demons and fear-based mindsets, which can feel a bit heavy.

But, once again, that initial heaviness and fear-based feelings eventually dissolve into love and light.

Set the intention to simply become aware of when you feel light and when you feel heavy.

Whenever you feel heavy, ask yourself *why*? Is it because you take fear-based actions that are out of alignment with who you are? Or is it because you take action to make others happy?

Or perhaps you experience that initial feeling of heaviness only because you're facing your inner demons? And learning the truth about the love and fear-based mindsets result in overwhelm?

Remember that, whatever happened, happened. You were a different person back then. But now, you can choose to make decisions out of love and design your life out of love!

Secret #3 Choosing Your Vibration

Most people choose to live in the past, and they allow harmful programs to control their lives. But now, you know you can choose to live with love.

From now on, choose to perceive your reality differently. Instead of thinking of the world as some random and cruel place that is against you and sends you unfavorable circumstances all the time ("Oh no, something is wrong with me, why do I always attract the negative!"), you can perceive whatever happens around you as feedback.

Many readers ask me: *OK, so, I've been living consciously, thinking, and acting positively. I'm aware of the negative patterns that used to hold me back, and I keep releasing them. I know I'm acting differently. Yet, quite often, I still experience the old situations and circumstances in my life. Why is that?*

First of all, there is always a delay from the Universe. Which explains why so many people give up on the Law of Attraction. They run out of patience to carry on changing their thoughts, feelings, and actions.

Let's say a person was in a negative, fear-based mindset all their life. Now, at forty-something years old, they are eager to change. And they do change. It's January the 1st, and as a part of their New Year's resolutions, they consciously apply love, light, and LOA.

Yet, a few months pass, it's now April, and even though a person feels better and more positive, their reality still hasn't changed that much.

Or perhaps it did shift, but not as much as they expected it to. And once again, everything is a choice. A person can choose to think that LOA doesn't work, and it wasn't worth it. All that time they put into reading and changing themselves, they could have just hung out at the bar and keep complaining about their life.

But at the same time, a person can choose to accept that whatever happens inside and around them is just feedback from the Universe! Negative emotions can be feedback. And unfavorable circumstances can also be feedback.

If you genuinely embrace LOA and a love-based mindset, you know and understand that real transformation takes time; you need patience.

At the same time, you need to consciously focus on the fact that you are continually getting signals from the Universe.

For example, you asked for money and abundance. You were excited to set up a new business; it all started so well. But then, a few months pass. You had a bad month, and your revenue went down.

You can choose to feel negative.

You can also use it as feedback from the Universe, such as: *perhaps I could create another stream of revenue for my business? Maybe there's another way I could use to attract clients? Could I use this situation as a motivation to improve my marketing?*

The light is always there if you're willing to look for it!

Let me share another example from my own life...

At the beginning of this year, I asked the Universe for energy and vibrant health because I wanted the strength and stamina to write several new books. Yet, a couple of months after I'd formulated my wish, I got very sick.

And yes, it's our human nature to automatically choose fear and complaining. For a few days, I began doubting myself, LOA, and my own teachings.

How can this be? I had a vision; I did everything that LOA tells us to do, and instead of vibrant health, I got the opposite?

But then, I decided to use my circumstances as feedback from the Universe. I understood that the Universe wanted me to slow down. I really had to take my health seriously.

I had to take a few months off, which seemed scary at first (after all, I wanted to manifest more money and abundance, which is why I asked for energy and health!). But eventually, I understood that it all happened for me, not to me. And now, a year after my initial request, I finally have the energy and vibrant health I wanted. I really had to learn to slow down.

I had to get sick first to get serious about my health and go on a holistic self-care journey. Now, I'm a different person. My health habits changed, my diet changed. In other words: my initial unfavorable circumstances lovingly forced me to take better care of myself.

I've seen similar patterns all over again, in different people who asked for love, abundance, health, or money and were given some kind of a test from the Universe.

Remember, whatever happens inside and around you, it's just feedback. And you can always consciously choose to raise your vibration by understanding that everything happens for you.

Rude boss? Well, you can now have more motivation to be a kind person and treat others with love.

Did you get sick? Well, your body is sending you an important message. It really needs some rest.

The relationship you're in is not what you hoped it would be. Well, perhaps now you genuinely understand the qualities of your dream partner?

Make it your daily mantra: *It all happens for me. Everything is unfolding just like it should.*

Some negative situations may sometimes manifest because of old, fear-based mindsets you held onto for so many years. It's OK, no judgment. It's just a reminder of how far you've come. Stick to love and light. All you have is the present moment. It's the present moment that creates a new, better future for you and your loved ones!

Secret #4 The Power of the Why Behind the Why

By embracing a love-based mindset, you become a conscious detective of your life. You always strive to find the root cause of any negativity or negative feeling in your life.

For example, you get late to work, because there was traffic. Most people would just say: *Oh, I'm having a bad day, and I guess my whole week will be like that.*

However, you can ask yourself: *why do I think I'm having a bad day? What happened?*

And you may start to uncover some answers such as:

I found the traffic very annoying because most people seemed so rude and uncaring. I felt like the whole world was against me, trying to make me late for work.

OK, so how exactly did I feel?

Well, I felt very powerless. No matter what I do, I can't get to work on time, and I feel stupid. Then, I'm late, and my boss and colleagues think I'm not serious. What if they laugh at me or tell me to leave?

Why would they ask me to leave if I'm never late to work, I'm good at what I do, there was an accident on the road, and for the first time in many years, I was fifteen minutes late?

Oh...because once as a teen, I missed the school bus and arrived late, and the teacher asked me to leave.

And from then on, he would never take me seriously...No matter how hard I studied.

BOOM! Now you can take a few deep breaths and allow yourself to be *authentically you* again. You are safe now. What happened, happened. Focus on the present moment. Nobody wants to put you down or make you leave. Instead, you were presented with a situation that helped you unpeel some negative emotions from the past and release old feelings of guilt.

Whenever you feel bad, use it as an opportunity to learn more about yourself and what triggers you. Play your own LOA detective! You're always learning more about yourself and the world around you!

Secret #5 Releasing Low Vibrations and Using Certainty for Your Highest Good

This little secret consists of two parts. The first one is based on understanding your emotional state and needs.

Your life is all about your emotional frequency. When you intend to create something in your life, you're going after a specific emotional state in reality.

If you manifest from an authentic state, you should access pure and honest vibrational energy.

For example, let's say you desire to manifest a new job and feel very passionate about it. You've researched the company you want to work for. You really love what they're doing and want to be a part of their team. Your energy is authentic. You feel good even before manifesting your desire. You feel excited, just thinking about it. At the same time, you already feel whole and complete. You're grateful for the work you're doing now and simply choose to upgrade your professional life from a place of love and excitement.

And with authentic energy, you manifest not only faster but also with joy and ease. What you manifest really makes you happy and transforms your life.

But, if your intentional energy is rooted in lack, you want to manifest to then feel whole and complete. It's a fear-based mindset because you assume that unless you don't manifest what you want, you can't feel happy. And so, you keep manifesting negative patterns of waiting and hoping for something to happen to then make you feel good and worthy.

Remove attachment by creating the feeling first. What emotional states are you trying to get through your manifestations? Can you feel them now?

When you think about your goal, what negative thoughts and voices come to your mind?

Create a pure connection by embracing all the positive and loved-based mindsets associated with your manifestation.

Let's say you want a beautiful house. At the same time, you want real, love-based friends who appreciate who you are. You also want financial security so that you don't need to worry about paying for the house.

Well, to create a union of good feelings and a clear signal for the Universe, you can visualize yourself in your dream house, with your dream friends, having a good time. You can then visualize yourself at your friends' houses. You all have lovely homes, it's normal for you. Nobody is jealous. All your friends are happy and abundant.

At the same time, if you try to manifest a new house, because right now you don't like your current one, or feel ashamed to invite your friends over...well... you're trying to manifest from a place of fear.

Or perhaps you want to manifest a beautiful house to feel significant? Well, why do you want to feel significant? Do you want to manifest from a place of love for a new home? Or do you fear that other people might think you're not good or successful enough unless you manifest something that impresses them?

Before intending to manifest anything, the bottom line is: you need to get rid of negative vibrations.

Negative vibrations come from fear. And to manifest our deepest desires, we need to step into unlimited love for ourselves, those around us, and our manifestations.

The second part of this secret is understanding your need for certainty while using it for your good, from a place of love.

Humans always want to feel safe to have something to count on. Our brain is always looking for ways to survive, not necessarily thrive or have an extraordinary life.

When you wake up and decide to live in expansion, you need to release the need for certainty if it comes from low vibrations and fear.

For example, people who get stuck in abusive relationships or jobs they hate often choose to stay where they are because it fulfills their need for certainty.

People who choose to eat fast food also do so because of certainty. There's a certainty of some flavors, maybe the need for sugar rush.

Now, there is nothing wrong with craving certainty.

Unless you choose a life of constant travel and adventure, you probably require certainty too. You want to make a certain amount of money a month. You want to know your work schedule. You want to be in a steady and loving relationship.

All you need to do is upgrade your needs; you can meet a need for certainty differently. You can find a new job that you love, and that also gives you confidence. You can have a loving partner that also fulfills your needs for certainty.

Your need for love and financial stability can be satisfied in a healthy, love-based way.

Revise your need for certainty. What's your next step? Is there a better, healthier way? There's always an answer.

Secret #6 Not All Negative Programming Is Really Negative

There's always good in bad. Most self-help and LOA literature talks about "programming" as something terrible, something we need to release at all costs. And yes, in most cases, it makes sense.

But we need to remember that there's negative programming as well as positive programming. Also, you may be running a good program for you and your current situation right now. However, it may turn out not to be longer beneficial for your new goals or levels of awareness in the future.

This is important to understand to save you negative feelings of shame and guilt!

There's a pattern amongst people who decide to do some inner work. They uncover negative patterns and programs that used to control their past behavior, and now they feel bad about themselves or start resenting other people.

Once again, remember, there's time to hold on, and there's time to let go. Perhaps you wanted to become an artist, and you realized that what was holding you back was a harmful program from the past. A relative told you that your work wasn't good enough. Now, you keep running that memory in your mind, feeling resentment toward that person and feeling guilty you took their words seriously.

Once again, don't torture yourself. There's no need to run the same situation in your mind over and over again. Maybe the family member had good intentions; they honestly said they thought that you weren't ready. They didn't say you weren't good enough but that your work back then wasn't good enough.

In other words, they had good intentions.

Now, it's up to you. You can turn that negative program into something positive; for example, *a family member tried to protect me from disappointment. They wanted me to practice more. They didn't want me to hear too many negative remarks from art critics.*

When you choose to transform negative into positive, your whole vibration changes. Now, you're genuinely empowered and can follow your path.

Or perhaps, you're running a program that you think is positive, but it turns out to be a bit misleading. You think you are already good enough to quit your job and become self-employed. When you were a kid, everyone always praised you for everything and was very supportive.

So, you keep running this program and quit your job, cold turkey. You feel confident you'll be able to make a good living as self-employed.

But it soon turns out that you can't find enough clients and aren't genuinely ready yet to be a full-time entrepreneur.

What you thought was a positive program turns out to be a bit negative because it doesn't get you closer to your goals. You realize you still don't have enough skills to make a living as a self-employed person.

And once again, you can resent your family because of the old programs they gave you ("you're the best," "you can do everything you want"). You can choose to feel like you've made a fool out of yourself.

Or you can mindfully decide to choose a new program. The old program you got from your family was useful for you when you were a kid. Your family had good intentions. They wanted you to feel confident enough to see what you were capable of.

Now, you can choose to feel thankful. At least you tested what it would feel like to be self-employed. Thanks to that, you now know what you need to focus on to succeed when you're ready to become a full-time entrepreneur.

The Universe gives you whatever vibration you're sending out. So, suppose you resent yourself and others because of some old program that turned out to be negative. In that case, the Universe will keep sending you more people, memories, and circumstances you can resent.

Release shame and guilt. Embrace the power of understanding. Stop criticizing yourself and others. Nobody is perfect. Yes, maybe your grandma gave you a negative belief about money, love, or something else. But, most likely, she had good intentions and wanted to protect you.

Explore your beliefs about money, love, career, friendships. Write down all the old, harmful programs, and simply set the intention to release them.

I also recommend you start practicing cord-cutting. You can cut cords with a person, feeling, old belief, and old energies that hold you back from living your full potential.

Even if you don't know the *what*, *who*, and *when*, you just feel like some negative energy is blocking you, but you don't know why, cord-cutting can also help you.

So, here's how you can cut cords with people, events, old timelines, feelings, objects, negative energies...whatever keeps you away from your vision!

Start by visualizing the individual, place, event, or feeling you wish to cut a cord with. Then, imagine scissors so that you can cut the cord.

(For example, if you continuously feel a negative feeling, and it keeps coming up in your visualizations, but you don't know whether it was a person who caused it, or perhaps an event, you can visualize the feeling, give it a color, shape or form and then cut cords with it).

Begin by connecting to the energy of the Divine — or the source.

Visualize the energetic cord that connects you with the low vibration entity you want to let go of.

Feel the energy that this entity is taking from you.

Now, set the intention to let go and visualize yourself cutting the cord between you and the negative entity using imaginary scissors.

Visualize the energetic cords recoil back.

Now, feel the recovery of energy and thank the other entity for their role in your life. Anchor that feeling of freedom and energy by pressing your thumb and index finger together.

To amplify this experience, you may choose to say (or think) the following words:

I now finally release all energetic cords because they no longer serve me.

I release you, and I remove me from these binds.

All cords are destroyed, across all dimensions, times, and planes, never to return.

I now banish these energetic cords and recover now all energy that was once lost.

My energy flows back to me, filling me once again with vitality and creating now a peaceful, energetic boundary of love and light.

Finish with some quiet time; you can meditate, lie down, or visualize something that makes you feel good. The main objective is to feel the energy that you have just reclaimed!

Think about it; you can now use this new, free energy to focus on what you want and manifest it into your dream reality!

Finally, visualize yourself being cloaked in a luminescent blanket of energetic protection. Feel the blanket all over your body.

This is your new energetic boundary!

Set an intention that this boundary remains in place as you step confidently forward into your day.

The next step is to re-write your beliefs. Awareness is everything!

I see so many people who get stuck in releasing old energies and negative beliefs or programs. Yet, instead of quickly replacing those old beliefs with some new, more empowering beliefs, they just spend all their time resenting their old selves.

The Universe likes to move fast. You need to practice releasing what no longer serves you while quickly replacing it with something new.

It's like getting rid of your old clothes. You also need to get some new ones, right? Unless you want to walk around naked, resenting some old-fashioned clothes, you are still "trying to get rid of."

After creating new beliefs, align your actions with them.

For example: *If now I choose to believe that money is safe and not evil, maybe I can scale my business?*

Finally, learning how Facebook ads work is fun and exciting. I no longer feel bad about expanding myself and my work.

I used to believe that putting myself out there with my work wasn't safe. But now, I have a new belief. I know that sharing my work is my purpose; it's who I am. And so, it's normal for me to take massive aligned action and follow my passion.

Or:

If I choose to believe that love is safe, and I can be loved for who I am, I no longer need to pretend I'm someone else. Now, I can just be myself and easily attract the man or woman of my dreams.

Secret#7 Release This Invisible Manifestation Killer

Do you have an invisible ceiling that makes you sabotage your actions?

For example, you think you're worthy and deserving of making a certain amount of money. You have a safe zone. But, you can't even think about expanding it.

Or, perhaps, you think love has a limit. Maybe you attracted a great partner, and things are marvelous, but you start thinking thoughts such as: *OK, it can't be that good, come on. I'm sure eventually he or she will stop treating me that well.*

And so, your fear-based mindsets create a reality of fear. Fear is fueled by contraction. In contrast, love is driven by expansion.

Think just like the Universe does. Don't be afraid to think big!

So many people choose to focus on the negative and get addicted to it. Example:
-*Now, it can only get worse*
-*When you start making money, it will not last forever*
-*The more you are in a relationship, the less love you feel for each other!*

Why choose to focus on going down if you can keep going up? The way you talk to yourself and others is essential. Stop expecting things to get worse and mindfully choose to expect them to get better.

Looking up and expanding your horizons doesn't mean you're not feeling grateful for what you have now. Yes, continue your gratitude for everything you have now.

But, at the same time, let the Universe know that you are open to receiving new levels of love, success, health, and happiness.

The Universe doesn't know any limits. So, choose to think as the Universe does, and stop feeling guilty for choosing to expand your horizons.

You like your job? Good! Because now, every day you love it more and more! You eat healthily and exercise?

Great! Now, every day it's more and more fun. Are you in love? Fantastic! Now, every day, you get to experience more and more of it.

Choosing to stick to your invisible limitations is like closing yourself in a basement. Why not expand instead?

Secret#8 The Liberating Essence of Letting Go

Most people try to let go, and they actually resist what they try to let go of. All their identity is focused on the act of letting go and releasing.

The real secret lies in understanding your emotions. We can't just sit still. We always rush, looking for the next thing to do. And so, we don't experience the present moment.

Every single feeling you have brings up different thoughts. The source is always the same, though- your core feeling or feelings.

For example, let's say you want to start a new business, and you get a thought: *oh, but what if I fail?*

That thought comes from the feeling of fear and anxiety (because of some past event).

Thoughts are just thoughts. But we all attached a feeling to it, based on our internal data, such as things that went wrong in the past, what we're not good at, or because someone else failed to do what we want to do.

Most of our suffering arises because we identify with our ego.

Emotion consists of a thought and feelings attached to it (based on past events). The unity of heart and mind creates our reality. But it's up to us to choose love instead of fear.

Something happens, we express what's happening, we become a part of that feeling, but the rest of it goes to our unconsciousness.

Any event is simply a trigger. The event in itself doesn't necessarily make you emotional.

For example, two people can get stuck in traffic. One can feel happy listening to their favorite songs and just intending to unwind or get in a good mood. But, other person chooses to complain, get angry, and indulge in low vibrations. Perhaps getting stuck in traffic makes them feel hopeless or triggers some traumatic experience. No judgment here.

When our feelings are too strong, we want to get unconscious by using food, TV, tobacco, scrolling on social media, being rude to other people, etc. We want to escape what's there, and we divert our attention outwards to not deal with anything.

We love suppressing and holding our feelings down. Escapism and suppression go hand in hand. Instead of feeling fear and surrendering it, we express it and replay it over and over again.

We also love repressing, which is unconscious. This is when old emotions get deep into the unconscious and keep boiling up until something triggers them.

Physical pain, insomnia, anxiety usually come because of repressed feelings. So, how to indeed release and be free from old fears haunting us?

Let's say you feel fearful.

You acknowledge the feeling first without any labels and resistance. You give yourself permission to fully feel it. There will be resistance, and you might feel a bit guilty for not suppressing it. Say: *I allow myself to handle this, with love, all from a place of love.*

Embrace that feeling fully. Finally, ask yourself: *Am I willing to let go and stop holding onto this feeling of fear, this grudge, this past experience?*

Even if you know the answer, please ask yourself several times: *am I really ready to let go?*

Real letting go is hard because we built our identities around it. Like I already mentioned, some people never let go. They are always stuck *trying* to let go. They are so used to hold on to their identity, and now, they try to let go without fully stepping into the new chapter of their lives. They still stick to an identity built around some old events or traumas. It's just now they do it from what they think is a better place (because they logically understand the concept of letting go).

When you finally let go, looking back at your past seems like looking at some past life or a different person.

Being triggered can be a good thing because now you know what you need to work on (as we said, such a trigger is just the feedback from the Universe).

There's nothing wrong with expressing how you feel or indulging in activities that make you feel good. But use them mindfully. Perhaps you like to watch a funny movie to laugh and have a good time, or you enjoy a glass of wine over a nice dinner with friends. However, you don't use these activities to escape your feelings.

Also, don't get stuck with labeling your judgments. And don't fear the fact that you're feeling fear. Instead, be mindfully grateful that now you have an awareness of the power of love.

Secret #9 Your Healthy, Love-Based Boundaries

To attract what you want, you need to mindfully protect yourself from what is holding you back. Luckily, there are many energy and mindset tools you can use. You can use love as your magic shield!

So why do you need personal boundaries? Well, look at anyone who has established success and wealth. All those people set healthy boundaries in their businesses, health, and personal life. Healthy boundaries are essential.

It's a skill you acquire as you grow. Sometimes you need to use masculine energy and force your new boundaries. If you are like me, an empath, you love helping people and giving, you may find it hard.

For example, I used to be always available on social media. I felt guilty if I couldn't reply to someone as soon as I saw their message. I thought I was on a mission to help everyone with everything. I totally ignored the fact that some people just wanted to pick my brains with no intention to ever purchase anything from me. Some didn't even intend to use my free information to improve their lives. They just wanted to chat or meet some people online. I felt terrible for not replying, and so I kept replying. Such a vicious cycle because I was always busy but not productive. Because of that, I neglected the most crucial activities (such as writing new books) to really help me grow.

I didn't have any energy left to write. I felt drained because of many energy vampires who wanted to take advantage of me. Of course, now, I don't blame them. I blame the fact that back then, I didn't have any healthy boundaries.

So, I had to learn it the hard way. I also realized that people on the other side didn't really understand that writing and publishing was something important to me. They thought I was doing it as a hobby. It's all because I didn't set boundaries and didn't consciously position myself and my brand.

I was acting out of fear: *"Oh, what will they think of me?"*. But, finally, I had to switch to loved-based boundaries. I had to create my schedule and stick to it. My main focus is writing, and I write for a particular reader avatar- curious and ambitious souls. These people appreciate my work and value my time (because they want me to write more!)

Then, after the most crucial writing and other publishing activities are accomplished, I check my email. There's no more stress or fear. I feel happy and balanced.

Now, all areas of life are interconnected. You need to understand your limitations. Suppose you always give up your boundaries in business/work. In that case, you may also get seduced by different temptations in health, such as indulging in fast food instead of cooking a healthy, wholesome meal.

For example, when I lacked boundaries in my professional life, I couldn't stick to a healthy lifestyle. Instead, I would get tempted to order pizza or some fast food.

So, ask yourself what makes you feel stressed and uncomfortable? Give yourself some time of honesty and think about what is right for you. Yes, I know for many of you it may seem a bit ego-based. But the truth is, if you want to help others, you need to help yourself first.

If you want freedom, you need a system. And you can't create a system when you lack boundaries and live in chaos.

People may leave you or your space when you set boundaries—no judgment, nothing wrong with them or you. By setting boundaries, you make it clear what your vibration is.

You can be the nicest person on this planet but still, have your boundaries. Anyone or anything that stresses you is unacceptable. Apply this rule across different areas of your life.

Tune into your feelings. In your gut, you know when something is wrong. Yes, you can excuse other people and keep justifying other people while slowly and surely start resenting them. You ignore your feelings, and eventually, resentment (which is very low vibration) is created.

Recognize your feelings early on. If you feel resentment towards yourself or other people, it means you didn't set your boundaries. Yes, allow yourself to feel annoyed. It's good that those feelings are coming out! Remember, it's just feedback. Ignoring your feelings means you are neglecting your existence. Act upon your feelings!

Discomfort and resentment (if it's more severe) indicate a lack of boundaries. Use it as feedback from the Universe and your higher self and do something about it.

What is your inner discomfort level? Give yourself an honest score (from one to ten). If you gave yourself seven or more, ask yourself what exactly is bothering you.

For example, you run a business, you hire people. You want to be a cool boss and allow your employees to be creative. You don't want to micromanage your team; you want to trust them. But then, a few months pass, and you realize you're not getting the results you wanted. You start feeling like a fool because your employees are taking advantage of you and your goodwill.

The real problem, though, is your lack of boundaries. As a person with healthy boundaries, you can communicate your vision and expectations and what is and isn't allowed—all in a kind, loved-based but firm way.

Switching to a loved-based mindset doesn't mean you must always agree with everyone. This can be a fear-based mindset. You feel scared to share how you really feel. So, keep your healthy boundaries and communicate them to others kindly.

The first step is forgiveness. It's all about learning. So, don't feel bad! Address your emotions first. Remember? Feelings are just feedback. Now you can mindfully change your reactions.

The second step is your communication. Be clear and specific and let other people know what they can and can't expect. People can't read your mind (unless they have some superpowers!)

Don't be afraid to protect yourself from negative energies. For example, I used to share too much about my business and private life, even with people I didn't know very well. I would just go on and on and explain everything that was going on, all with good intention. But then, I realized that some people would either get jealous or gossip. So, I had to learn to keep certain things to myself. I had to understand who I could confide in. Now, when someone I don't really know that well asks me about some specific business stuff or numbers, I politely say: *"Well, I only share this information with my accountant and the tax office, of course."* And we both start laughing!

When someone I hardly know asks me about my personal life, I like to answer with humor: *"Oh, it's OK, but probably wouldn't make a good soap opera."*

As a self-employed person working from home, I also had to set my work and life balance boundaries. Firstly, I had to set them with myself. I know this may seem weird to so many people who just get up and drive to their workplace.

But I also know that those working from home may sometimes struggle with their schedule and boundaries. And now, with the post lockdown reality, more and more people are forced to work from home.

So, once again, I had to use my masculine energy to develop a specific schedule. Wake up at a particular time, get the most important writing and business stuff done early in the morning.

Then, I had to communicate my boundaries and schedule to my family. I explained to them that working for myself doesn't mean I'm always free and available and that if I don't stick to my schedule, I won't be successful.

I also got two different phone numbers, one for work, another for my family. So, now, when I switch from work, I'm available for my family. Since I'm more productive during the week and follow my schedule, I can enjoy life-work balance and unwind on weekends and be fully present for my family and friends, instead of worrying I have so much to do.

Keep auditing yourself. This work never ends. Keep observing your behaviors and boundaries, as well as the way you communicate them to others.

You may realize that you're affected by the way you were raised and your family's role. For example: *to be a good daughter, I have to behave in a certain way.*

Perhaps some family members can always influence or convince you to do something because they know your weaknesses?

Be aware that some people may be taking advantage of you (doesn't mean they are bad people, but they just got used to specific patterns). Are you in *give and take* relationships, or is it *only give give give*?

Also, be mindful and respect other people's boundaries and preferences.

I recently found myself feeling lots of resentment towards my younger sister. It got triggered during a conversation we had about business. I was very excited to share a new idea I got after reading one of my favorite love-based marketing authors. And my sister said something like: *"Don't even compare yourself to this author. She is on a much higher level. You're not really that successful. So, I'm not too sure this could work for you."*

At first, it really hurt me. I had a good intention and just wanted to share some ideas that I knew could help my sister. I wasn't comparing myself to anyone. What really triggered me is the fact that I always shared everything I learned with my sister. She's now pretty successful in her business because of one idea I shared with her a few years ago while giving her the exact steps to follow. So, feeling a bit sad, I thought to myself: "I helped her so much, and now, instead of gratitude, I'm getting some mixed messages!"

But then, after diving more in-depth, I realized a few things:
-my sister was in lots of stress because her health wasn't very good; she was on medication and in lots of pain. And I chose to talk about business, which probably made her a bit tired. She was on holiday and wanted to unwind. She even told me she didn't want to talk about work or business, but I just kept talking.
-when we were kids, our parents would always compare her to me ("you should learn from Elena, she was always good at geography," "why did you get a C minus? Elena was always an A or B student, maybe she can help you with your exam?")

And yes, our parents had good intentions too. But once again, childhood and adulthood are two different journeys.

One needs to learn to let go. Some patterns and behaviors might have been helpful to us at some point when we were kids. But now, they can irritate us and cause us discomfort.

When setting and respecting boundaries for ourselves, we must also respect other people's boundaries. In my case, I didn't respect my sister's wishes and boundaries. I kept talking about topics she didn't want to talk about, therefore triggering a somehow ironic response.

It all ended up well. We're all right now. But we had to have an honest family conversation to ensure everyone was OK and everyone was treating everyone else well. No irony and no passive-aggressive remarks!

To sum up this story, you should never tolerate any negative remarks you get from your family and friends.

But also ask yourself what triggered them. Did you respect their boundaries? Were you empathic? Do you actually understand where they're coming from?

Healthy boundaries also prevent burnout. Now, to clarify where I stand on taking action - if you've read any of my previous books, you know I'm all about taking action. I don't believe in just sitting around, mindlessly repeating your wishes and waiting for them to magically materialize. I'm all for taking mindful, aligned action to show the Universe that you're committed.

But at the same time, I'm not for *hustle hustle hustle* mentality. Yes, it may work for some people, which is excellent. Everyone is different.

This is where your personal boundaries come up. You need to decide what works for you long-term. For example, if I took action based entirely on what other people do, I'd burn out.

I used to stress out about pushing harder and tried to sleep less to get more done. I followed young people who could easily do with five or six hours of sleep. But my body rebelled.

I knew I needed more rest. So, I no longer feel guilty about sleeping more. I know I need eight to nine hours of sleep, and some time to fall asleep, meditate and unwind. I like to wake up feeling well-rested.

In other words, I honor my self-care and my feelings. And I base my self-care on what I need to do, not on what others are doing. And not on the latest trend (as for what we must eat, do, and how to sleep).

Now I'm in a better place, and I can be a better friend, family member, and entrepreneur. I no longer feel guilty about setting up some *me* time.

Ask yourself, how often do you replenish your energy with loved-based boundaries so that you can experience love-based vibrations and manifest faster?

Secret #10 When Making Mistakes is Important If You Want to Attract Abundance

Many people say if you keep repeating failure, it's probably a negative pattern. And yes, it's definitely true.

We already know that negative situations and patterns are feedback.

But at the same time, if you've read any biography of successful people, you will quickly realize that they failed a lot!

They see failures as a lesson, not a mistake. From an energetic level, it's interesting to look at negative patterns around each so-called "failure" and do some energy work with a healer to remove trapped negative energy. I'm all for energy work!

But from a pure mindset level, in our case, love-based mindset…

It's all about learning! Looking back on my journey as an entrepreneur, I regret that I didn't fail more. Because I know that all the success and abundance I could attract was because I could learn from my mistakes.

I could write an entire book talking about projects I tried and failed with. But looking back, all those past experiences made me wiser and stronger. They helped me change my brain so that now I can make better decisions.

I've failed in different ventures (as self-employed) and various jobs I tried for various companies in multiple sectors.

For a long time, I felt very ashamed because I couldn't stick to one path successfully. And yes, I did lots of energy work desperately trying to get rid of negative energy. Nothing wrong with energy work.

But the best energy work is when you combine it with mindset work (and vice versa). Energy work is working with your heart; mindset work is more about working with your head. In this physical world, we need both.

So, I gave myself permission to make mistakes! I decided to own the fact that I had the privilege to work in different sectors. I felt grateful I tried different jobs and businesses and learned a lot as a result.

Are you an ambitious soul who dreams about attracting incredible abundance? Do you want to build an internationally recognized company? Perhaps you want to become a famous author, artist, or self-employed professional. Well, whatever your dreams are, you need to be OK with making mistakes. Use them to learn as much as you can.

The same rule applies to other areas of your life. Perhaps you desire to attract a loving partner. Yet, you got stuck in a vicious cycle of attracting people you find negative. Well, at least now you know what you don't like, and so, you can set an intention to attract precisely the opposite, in a healthy, love-based way.

You want vibrant health. In alignment with that, you try different diets. Yet they all fail! Well, at least now, you know what not to do. And so, you can simplify your wellness quest by creating your own diet!

Perhaps you want to follow your passion and become a blogger. You put in lots of work learning how the online world works. You keep creating valuable content. Yet you can't grow your following because you realize you didn't choose the right niche and feel stuck. Well, at least now, you know how blogging works. You can now set a new blog in a new category and do it much better!

Remember, you don't fail, you succeed or you learn. So, be passionate about learning. As you stay open to learning, you also open yourself to receiving new signs from the Universe! Everything is unfolding as it should! Eliminate the word "failure" from your vocabulary. Instead, be curious about learning and growing!

Personal Message from Elena

Thank You so much for reading this book to the very end! I hope you found it inspiring and discovered at least one helpful idea to help you grow on your Law of Attraction journey.

If you have a few minutes, I'd really appreciate it if you could leave me a short review on Amazon. Let other LOA readers in our community know who this book can help and why.

Thank You Thank You Thank You,
I hope we "meet" again,
Much love,

Elena

For more information and resources about LOA, please visit my website:

www.LOAforSuccess.com

If you'd like to say hi, please email me at elena@LOAforSuccess.com

Free LOA Newsletter + Bonus Gift

To help you AMPLIFY what you've learned in this book, I'd like to offer you a free copy of my *LOA Workbook – a powerful, FREE 5-day program (Ebook & audio)* designed to help you raise your vibration while eliminating resistance and negativity.

To sign up for free, visit the link below now:

www.loaforsuccess.com/newsletter

You'll also get free access to my highly acclaimed, uplifting **LOA Newsletter.**

Through this email newsletter, I regularly share all you need to know about the manifestation mindset and energy.

My newsletter alone helped hundreds of my readers manifest their own desires.

Plus, whenever I release a new book, you can get it at a deeply discounted price or even for free.

You can also start receiving my new audiobooks published on Audible at no cost!

To sign up for free, visit the link below now:

www.loaforsuccess.com/newsletter

I'd love to connect with you and stay in touch with you while helping you on your LOA journey!

If you happen to have any technical issues with your sign up, please email us at:

support@LOAforSuccess.com

More Books by Elena G. Rivers

Money Mindset: Stop Manifesting What You Don't Want and Shift Your Subconscious Mind into Money & Abundance

How Not to Manifest: Manifestation Mistakes to Avoid and How to Finally Make LOA Work for You

Visualization Demystified: The Untold Secrets to Re-Program Your Subconscious Mind and Manifest Your Dream Reality in 5 Simple Steps

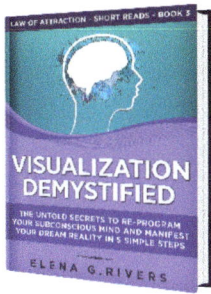

Law of Attr-Action for Entrepreneurs: Advanced Identity Shifting Secrets to Manifest the Income & Impact You Deserve

www.ingramcontent.com/pod-product-compliance
Lightning Source LLC
Chambersburg PA
CBHW040420100526
44589CB00021B/2775